Do Lizards Eat Ice Cream?

How Animals Beat the Heat

For Benjamin and Lianna, with lots of hugs and kisses — E.K.
To Kevin, Chester, and my amazing family — J.P.

Text © 2020 Etta Kaner
Illustrations © 2020 Jenna Piechota

Owlkids Books acknowledges the financial support of the Canada Council for the Arts, the Ontario Arts Council, the Government of Canada through the Canada Book Fund (CBF) and the Government of Ontario through the Ontario Creates Book Initiative for our publishing activities.

Published in Canada by
Owlkids Books Inc.
1 Eglinton Avenue East
Toronto, ON M4P 3A1

Published in the United States by
Owlkids Books Inc.
1700 Fourth Street
Berkeley, CA 94710

Library of Congress Control Number: 2019956955

Library and Archives Canada Cataloguing in Publication

Title: Do lizards eat ice cream? : how animals beat the heat / written by Etta Kaner ; illustrated by Jenna Piechota.
Names: Kaner, Etta, author. | Piechota, Jenna, illustrator.
Description: Follow up to Do frogs drink hot chocolate?
Identifiers: Canadiana 20200183869 | ISBN 9781771473989 (hardcover)
Subjects: LCSH: Body temperature—Regulation—Juvenile literature. | LCSH: Animal heat—Juvenile literature. | LCSH: Heat adaptation—Juvenile literature.
Classification: LCC QP135 K383 2020 | DDC j571.7/61—dc23

Edited by Sarah Harvey
Designed by Danielle Arbour

Manufactured in Guangdong Province, Dongguan City, China, April 2020, by Toppan Leefung Packaging & Printing (Dongguan) Co., Ltd.
Job #BAYDC79

A   B   C   D   E   F   G

Publisher of Chirp, Chickadee and OWL | Owlkids Books is a division of bayard canada
www.owlkidsbooks.com

Do Lizards Eat Ice Cream?

How Animals Beat the Heat

Written by **Etta Kaner**

Illustrated by **Jenna Piechota**

Owlkids Books

When it gets hot out, do animals wear flip-flops?

So how do they beat the heat?
Let's find out...

Do lizards eat ice cream
to beat the heat?

NO!

Shovel-snouted lizards dance to cool down. Yes, dance! After racing around on the burning sand looking for food, they stop to dance. The lizard lifts up its front foot and opposite back foot at the same time. Then it switches to the other two feet. This way, air gets underneath to cool the feet.

Do koalas run through sprinklers?

NO!

Koalas hug trees to keep cool. Lower branches are cooler than the surrounding air. So koalas snuggle up close to a low branch. The thinner fur on their bellies helps koalas feel the coolness of the branch.

Do sea stars drink a lot of water?

Ochre sea stars live near the seashore. When the water goes out at low tide, the sea stars are stuck on land. To prepare for this, they fill up with cold seawater so they won't dry out in the sun. Imagine if you had to drink thirty cups of cold water before heading outside!

Do desert ants sit in front of air conditioners?

Desert ants need to find food and then get out of the heat fast. Their super long legs (for an ant!) help them do this. By taking longer steps, the ants can move quickly. Plus, their legs raise their bodies away from the hot sand, keeping them cooler.

Do elephants use fans?

Elephants have huge ears with lots of blood vessels. When they flap their ears, they create a breeze. This cools the blood in the ears. The cooler blood then returns to the rest of the body. Ahh, now that feels better!

Do lungfish take naps?

YES!

African lungfish live in water that often dries up and turns to mud. When this happens, it's time for a nap. The lungfish digs a burrow under the mud and covers itself with a blanket of bubbles. When does it wake up? When it rains. But that could take as long as two years to happen!

Do alligators wear shades?

NO!

Alligators do need to shade their eyes from the sun. But not with sunglasses! Their eyes, like yours, have pupils that let in light. But alligator pupils are slit-shaped, like a keyhole. In the bright sun, the slits narrow to block out most of the sunlight.

Do kangaroos wear sun hats?

Kangaroos lick their forearms to stay cool. They cover them with lots of saliva. When the saliva evaporates, the forearms cool off, and so does the rest of the body. You cool off in the same way when your sweat evaporates. No need to lick yourself!

Do frogs use sunscreen?

YES!

Waxy monkey tree frogs make their own sunscreen. It comes from glands in their skin. They use their legs to rub a waxy cream all over their body. The "frog sunblock" stops the frog's skin from drying out. This is one frog that doesn't mind the sun!

Do plovers take cool showers to beat the heat?

YES!
(SORT OF)

On hot, sunny days, Egyptian plovers cool their eggs by keeping them wet. How? Mom and Dad go back and forth to a nearby river to soak their belly feathers. Then they take turns sitting on the eggs. They keep this up even after the chicks have hatched!

Do oxen get haircuts?

NO!

Musk oxen have long, straggly outer hair with a layer of soft, warm wool underneath. This undercoat is great for winter but too hot for summer. So every spring, musk oxen shed their cozy undercoat. No need to go to a barber!

Do squirrels carry umbrellas?

Cape ground squirrels have long, bushy tails that they use like umbrellas. As they look for food under the hot desert sun, they raise their tails over their bodies for shade.

Do gulls wear white to beat the heat?

YES!
(SORT OF)

Herring gull nests can get very hot because they are out in the open. So when herring gulls sit on their eggs, they turn their bodies to face the sun. The white feathers of their head, neck, and breast soak up less heat than the dark back feathers.

All of the animals in this book have special ways to beat the heat.

But what about you?
What do YOU do when it gets hot?